BIG Q

ARE
SCIENCE
AND
CHRISTIAN
FAITH
AT ODDS?

HOLMAN®
REFERENCE
NASHVILLE, TENNESSEE

Big Questions: Are Science and Christian Faith at Odds?
Copyright 2021 Holman Bible Publishers
Nashville, Tennessee. All Rights Reserved.

All Scripture quotations are taken from the Christian Standard Bible®, Copyright
© 2017 by Holman Bible Publishers.

CSB Apologetics Study Bible, Copyright © 2017 by Holman Bible Publishers.
CSB Worldview Study Bible, Copyright © 2018 by Holman Bible Publishers.

Printed in China
1 2 3 4 5 6   24 23 22 21
RRD

Contents

INTRODUCTION

One doesn't typically hear the word *apologetics* in the everyday vernacular of Christians today. The term is derived from a Greek word meaning "a defense." Thus, engaging in Christian apologetics simply means providing a Christian defense of the faith. Or, to say it another way, it involves giving an intellectual defense of *why* we believe *what* we believe.

The apostle Peter writes, "But in your hearts regard Christ the Lord as holy, ready at any time to give a defense to anyone who asks you for a reason for the hope that is in you" (1Pt 3:15). Peter, along with other writers of Scripture, knew the importance of being able to offer reasons to others regarding our belief in Christ or the Christian worldview in general. If asked why we believe any tenet of biblical doctrine, Christians ought to be able to give coherent reasons for that belief.

But not only does apologetics help us to defend our beliefs, it is also helps us to strengthen the faith we have—to bolster it, to assure us that our beliefs are in fact reasonable. This means that apologetics isn't merely a mental exercise for thinking deeply and critically about matters. Instead, it is another discipline of the Christian life that helps increase our love for and devotion to God as we seek to know him and make him better known to others.

The Big Questions series serves these two purposes for the reader. It provides reasons and evidence on select topics to both strengthen Christian faith and to help one articulate that faith to others. Curated from the *Apologetics Study Bible* and *Worldview Study Bible*, the content in this booklet will equip you in your journey toward being better grounded in your faith and better equipped at sharing it.

— *Andy McLean*

ARE SCIENCE AND CHRISTIANITY AT ODDS?

Andy McLean

In order to assess whether science is somehow at odds
or incompatible with Christian belief, it is important
to first get a better handle on what science is—a task
that is actually more difficult than most people realize.
For starters, science is one of those things that is nearly
impossible to define. There are some standard entry-level
textbooks that simply try to define science in accordance
with the scientific method of investigating the natural
world, using skills like observation and experimentation.
However, while it is helpful to turn to the standard
method used among many scientists, unfortunately this

doesn't help much given that not all of the sciences use the same methods. Cosmologists, astronomers, geologists, biologists, microbiologists, chemists, biochemists, and physicists all explore different parts of creation using different methods. This is because the nature of what is studied will always determine the method with which it is studied.

Of course, there is nothing problematic or contradictory even here—Christians too can affirm the fact that the subject of one's study will determine the method of how it is studied. If biology requires a different set of skills when it comes to observation and experimentation, then it won't come as a surprise to learn that theology, or the study of God, will require an altogether different medium given the different subject of that study.

Thus, from a methodological perspective, there is nothing necessarily unsettling between Christianity and science, a point that has been widely acknowledged even in the history of science itself. In fact, anyone looking at the history of science will see that modern-day science was born out of the Christian worldview. Scientists, such as Copernicus, Francis Bacon, Johannes Kepler, Galileo, Descartes, Pascal, Isaac Newton, Robert Boyle, Gregor Mendel, and William Thomson Kelvin, just to name a few, believed that a Christian worldview provided the very intellectual foundation for science to be practiced given the Christian belief that an intelligent God designed and created a rationally ordered universe that could be understood by humans. Indeed, the very fact that the order and design of the universe can be rightly understood by our human faculties is an amazing thing—one that is best explained by the Christian doctrine of humanity being created in the image of God, possessing the same rational capacity that is seen in the natural world. If things were not orderly, then there would be no regularity within nature, and if no regularity, then science would not be possible.

The rich history between science and Christianity undermines any blanket notions that the two entities stand in contradiction to one another. This warfare thesis that the truth claims being made from both sides are at odds or irreconcilable are grossly misstated and fail to reflect the mutual support the two sides have enjoyed over the course of history. Now, that isn't to say that there aren't some specific ethical concerns or specific positions within the mainstream scientific community that may conflict with certain beliefs and doctrines in the Christian faith, and that need to be addressed. In fact, some of the remaining chapters in this booklet will address those specific concerns. However, those examples don't represent the scientific enterprise as a whole, nor even the position of all scientists within those fields. When an instance of apparent conflict arises and seems to intersect with a particular Christian doctrine or stance, then those examples can and should be addressed on a case-by-case basis. But what is important is the recognition that, despite what many people believe, science or the particular scientific positions in those cases are not only making inferences that could be wrong, but are also limited in what they can actually claim to be true.

To say it another way, the facts that science observes and examines are not self-interpreting. Think of it this way: The things we observe within nature, the things we see and feel and examine under microscopes, are the things we call the facts. Think about a crime scene investigator arriving at the scene of a homicide. He might look at the condition of the house the victim is in (Is it trashed with signs of forced entry? Or does it look like nothing has been touched?), the condition and position of the body (Was there a struggle?), the presence or absence of a murder weapon, and any evidence of human presence in the home (fingerprints, DNA evidence, etc.). All of the things that he looks at are the "facts," the things he has to work with. But if you think about it, the facts are not self-interpreting. It takes a mind to piece together the facts and draw proper inferences, such as the possibility that the victim must have known his attacker because there are no signs of forced entry and no signs of a struggle.

This is what we mean when we say that facts are not self-interpreting. In order to make sense, they require an intelligent mind, and that mind may or may not arrive at the right conclusions. The reason why we don't always reason correctly or draw all the right inferences is because we bring with us our own sets of assumptions or presuppositions when looking at the evidence. We constantly do this in all spheres of life, and the same is true when it comes to doing science. Not only do the facts not interpret themselves, but we too, as observers, have to be careful to not bring the wrong presuppositions to the scientific process. For instance, if we were to begin our science with the presupposition that God doesn't exist and that everything within nature can be explained by other natural processes (this is called "methodological naturalism," which many scientists use all the time), then from the very outset we have rendered it impossible to even consider some potential explanations. If we have the presupposition that only mindless matter exists, then we are forced to exclude from the start any notion of God or his intervention within human history. But this, of course, isn't science. This is an atheistic worldview trying to use science for its own advantage. Instead, science follows the evidence where the evidence leads, whether pointing to the natural or perhaps even the supernatural.

Science is not an enemy of Christianity—it never has been nor is it today. Even atheist Stephen Jay Gould, widely regarded as America's greatest evolutionary biologist, was adamant that his own skepticism could not be derived from the sciences. He says, "To say it for all my colleagues and for the umpteenth million time . . . science simply cannot (by its legitimate methods) adjudicate the issue of God's possible superintendence of nature. We neither affirm nor deny it; we simply can't comment on it as scientists."

In other words, those who argue that science disproves God have gone beyond the bounds of legitimate science, and instead are simply disguising their atheistic beliefs as science. In fact, those who abuse science in this way are ignoring what scientific evidence is making more and more clear—that the order and mathematical precision displayed in nature, particularly when it comes to the fine-tuning conditions necessary to sustain life on our planet, are indeed highly suggestive of the fact that our universe is not here by chance or necessity, but instead is the result of a purposeful design.

WHAT IS THE RELATIONSHIP BETWEEN SCIENCE AND THE BIBLE?*

J. P. Moreland

C hristians are committed to the reality of knowable truths from the Bible and science. Further, Christians seek to integrate claims from both sources into their worldview. How is this done? What is the relationship between the Bible and science?

Some claim that the history of Bible-science interaction is largely a war, with theology constantly losing. But for two reasons, this claim is false. First, the relationship

---

* Originally published in the *CSB Apologetics Study Bible* under the same title.

between the Bible and science is much richer than what can be captured by a warfare metaphor (see below). Second, many times the teachings of the Bible and science confirm each other, and when there have been differences it is not always the Bible that has been reexamined. Sometimes scientific claims have been reinterpreted. For example, shortly after Darwinism arose, creationists predicted that there would be gaps in the fossil record, with no clear transition forms, whereas evolutionists predicted that thousands of transitional forms would be discovered. Evolutionists were wrong.

In general, the warfare metaphor is not adequate. At least five different models have been offered to capture the integration of science and the Bible. None of these positions is exhaustive, and one can subscribe to any of the five on a case-by-case basis.

1. *Distinct realms.* Claims from the Bible and science may involve two distinct, nonoverlapping areas of investigation. For example, debates about angels or the extent of the atonement have little to do with organic chemistry. Similarly, it is of little interest to theology

whether a methane molecule has three or four hydrogen atoms in it.

2. *Complementary descriptions of the same realm.* Claims from the Bible and science may involve two different, complementary, noninteracting approaches to the same reality. Sociological aspects of church growth and some psychological aspects of conversion may involve scientific descriptions of certain phenomena that are complementary to a theological description of church growth or conversion. Claims in chemistry that water comes from combining hydrogen and oxygen are complementary to theological claims that God providentially creates water.

In general, we may describe God's activity in terms of primary causes (when God acts in an unusual way and directly, miraculously produces an effect) or secondary causes (when God acts in ordinary ways by sustaining and using natural processes to accomplish a result). The complementarity approach is most effective when God acts by way of secondary causes.

3. *Direct interaction.* Claims from the Bible and science may directly interact such that either one area

of study offers rational support for the other or one area of study raises rational difficulties for the other. For example, certain theological teachings about the existence of the soul raise rational problems for scientific claims that deny the existence of the soul. The general theory of evolution raises various difficulties for certain ways of understanding the book of Genesis. Some have argued that the second law of thermodynamics supports the theological proposition that the universe had a beginning. Special creationism—for example, young-earth and progressive creationism—are applications of this approach to the question of the origin and development of life.

4. *Presuppositional interaction.* Biblical teaching can be used to support the presuppositions of science. Some have argued that many of the presuppositions of science (e.g., the existence of truth; the rational, orderly nature of reality; the adequacy of our sensory and cognitive faculties as tools suited for knowing the external world) make sense and are easy to justify through Christian theism but are without justification in a worldview that does not include God.

5. **Practical application.** Biblical teaching can help one practically apply principles discovered in science and vice versa. For example, theology teaches that fathers should not provoke their children to anger; psychology can add important details about what this means by offering information about family systems, the nature and causes of anger, etc. Psychology can devise various tests for assessing whether one is or is not a mature person, given a normative definition (a definition of what ought to be the case and not just a description of what actually is the case) from the Bible as to what a mature person ought to be like.

It is the direct interaction approach that opens up the possibility that scientific and biblical claims may provide mutual intellectual support or be in conflict with one another.

Three things should be kept in mind in approaching areas of apparent conflict.

First, the vast majority of biblical teachings and scientific claims have little to do with each other directly, and it is wrong to give the impression that most of the issues from these two sources support or conflict with each other. Areas of potential conflict are quite small compared to the vastness of ideas from the Bible and science.

Second, there are several areas where scientific discoveries have lent support to biblical assertions:

- evidence that the universe had a beginning
- evidence that the universe is fine-tuned and delicately designed so that life could appear
- evidence strongly suggesting that there is no naturalistic explanation for the origin of life and moreover that life is characterized by information that always comes from a mind
- evidence that living things are irreducibly complex such that all their parts need each other to function and thus could not have evolved gradually
- numerous archaeological confirmations of biblical claims
- psychological discoveries of the importance of a unified spiritual, moral free agent to explain human functioning and maturity.

Third, we should face areas of conflict honestly but confidently in light of points one and two. Christians

ought to make sure we have understood scriptural and
scientific data correctly, and we should seek solutions
that are both biblically and scientifically adequate. Given
that Christianity provides a reasonable worldview for
justifying science, that most areas of science and the
Bible do not directly interact, and that many scientific
discoveries have added confirmation to biblical teaching,
there is no reason why Christians cannot be rational
in admitting that there are currently areas of apparent
conflict for which we do not have adequate solutions.
No worldview is without some problems and unresolved
questions. Still, contrary to popular opinion, the
difficulties that scientific claims raise for biblical teaching
are far from overwhelming, and they are fewer in number
than one would expect by listening to propagandists from
secular culture.

WHAT ARE SOME MODELS FOR RELATING SCRIPTURE AND SCIENCE?*

Jimmy H. Davis

B oth the Scriptures and science have a story to tell. From the creeds and systematic theology that result from study of Scripture, we have the metanarrative (grand, all-encompassing story) of God as Creator who prepared and sustains a pleasant world for humans. Both that world and its inhabitants have come under a curse due to sin, the Bible teaches, but history will end in the triumphant return of Christ as King of kings and Lord of lords.

* Originally published in the *CSB Worldview Study Bible* under the title "Models for Relating Scripture and Science."

The current metanarrative of science is the story of the Big Bang, drawing on evidence from physics that suggests that about 13.7 billion years ago space and time appeared instantaneously from nothing in an infinitely small and infinitely hot singularity. As the universe expanded and cooled, there appeared atoms, stars, galaxies, planets, life, and finally humans.

Concordism and Non-Concordism

The many approaches that biblical and scientific scholars have used to relate Scripture and science can be collected into two overarching approaches: concordism and non-concordism.

Concordism is derived from the word "concord," which means harmony or agreement between persons, groups, or things. Scholars who favor concordism believe that exegesis (interpretation) of the Scriptures reveals a message that is in harmony with correct understandings of modern science. This means that any time the Bible addresses a science-related issue, it does so with full accuracy. Concordism is sometimes expressed in terms of the two books of God (nature and Scripture), which will be in harmony when both are properly interpreted.

The non-concordist model does not see a harmony between the biblical testimony and the well-supported conclusions of science. Non-concordists believe this lack of harmony is due to the fact that in Scripture God never sought to speak in terms of literally correct science but instead chose to speak in accordance with ancient non-scientific ways of describing nature. Non-concordists who are not Christians would likely say that the Bible tried but failed to speak accurately about scientific topics. In the first approach, the Bible's failure to speak with scientific accuracy is taken as the expected result of God speaking in a comprehensible manner to people living prior to the scientific revolution. In the second approach, the Bible's failure to speak with scientific accuracy is seen as proof that the Bible does not have a divine author—a skeptical viewpoint that unreasonably expects God to speak in accordance with his full knowledge rather than using "baby talk" when speaking to finite, historically-situated humans.

Varieties of Concordism

There are many types of concordism, with a major dividing issue being the meaning of the Hebrew word for "day" (*yom*) in Genesis (1:3,8,13,19,23,31; 2:2). One group, known as creation science or young earth creationism (YEC), interprets *yom* in Genesis to mean a literal twenty-four-hour day. This stance is closely tied to "evening" and "morning" being referenced alongside each use of "day" in the opening creation narrative. Advocates of the young-earth view attempt to find harmony between this exegesis and the narrative of science. The YEC approach requires major modification to the standard scientific understanding of the fields of astronomy, physics, biology, and geology. Australian-born Ken Ham promotes YEC through his organization, Answers in Genesis. One of their staple beliefs is that science must be submitted to a literal reading of Genesis.

Another group, known as creationism or old earth creationism (OEC), adopts a different understanding of the word *yom*, which leads them to conclude that in the Genesis creation accounts it refers to a period of time longer than twenty-four hours. According to the OEC approach, each creation day was a long period of time that involved many acts of creation by God. The non-literal use of "day" in Genesis 2:4, where it refers to the "day" in which God "made the earth and the heavens," is a key textual basis for claiming that "day" does not always refer to a twenty-four-hour period. The OEC approach sees more harmony with standard scientific understanding of the history of the universe than does the YEC approach, though it resists the naturalistic presuppositions that often creep into popular science theories. Canadian-born astronomer Hugh Ross is a leading promoter of OEC through his organization, Reasons to Believe. Staple beliefs of this and other OEC organizations include that science is not made futile by our fall into sin and that the Bible actually contains allusions or hints to scientific truths such as the Big Bang and an ancient earth.

Varieties of Non-concordism

The non-concordist approach results from a different exegesis of the Scriptures, which states that the Bible's intention is not to teach science but that the Bible uses the language of science and natural history to aid our understanding of spiritual truths.

The *framework view* is a non-concordist approach that proposes that the days of Genesis are literary devices used to convey important truths about purpose and ultimate origin. In this view, God's creative activity as recounted in Genesis is arranged in a topical, non-sequential manner and does not intend to make any claims about the age of the universe. The six creation days form a symmetrically arranged, topical account of creation, set in two triads with similar activities in each triad. God is seen creating three kingdoms in the first triad: Day One (Gn 1:3–5), light; Day Two (Gn 1:6–8), sea and sky; and Day Three (Gn 1:9–13), earth and plants. In the second triad, God populates these kingdoms with their rulers: Day Four (Gn 1:14–19), luminaries; Day Five (Gn 1:20–23), fish and birds; and Day Six (Gn 1:24–31), animals and mankind. Finally, Day Seven (Gn 2:1–3) is a Sabbath for the Creator King. Some see this triad arrangement in the seven-lamp menorah of the Jewish temple (Ex 25:31–40).

In summary, the framework view holds that the narrative of Genesis is not meant to provide a literal scientific account of God's creative methods, nor the time frame in which he created. Rather, it asserts that Genesis was intended to combat polytheism and pantheism. The message is that God is the Creator of all things; questions about how or when he created are seen as irrelevant. The late American theologian and OT scholar Meredith G. Kline was a proponent of the framework view.

Another non-concordist approach is called *complementarity*, which states that science and theology complement each other to provide a complete picture of reality. Science and theology do not rival each other but, when properly interpreted, provide valid information about the same thing. Science may have a rational narrative for the history of the universe, for instance, but cannot explain why the laws underlying this narrative are fine-tuned for humans. The spiritual truth of the creation narrative in Genesis completes this picture of nature by providing a framework to understand the fine-tuning in terms of the creative and providential work of a loving God. English physicist and theologian John Polkinghorne promoted complementarity in his writings.

Summary

Each of the above models of relating Scripture and science are held by devout Christians. Some scholars even hold views that draw on several of the models. This side of eternity, we will probably never acquire enough knowledge to know indisputably the best way to relate these two great ways of knowing (Scripture and science). As Paul says in 1 Corinthians 13:12, "For now we see only a reflection as in a mirror, but then face to face. Now [we] know in part, but then [we] will know fully, as [we are] fully known."

HAVE DARWINISM AND DAWKINS DISPROVED GOD?*

Stephen C. Meyer

Recently many prominent—and self-appointed—spokesmen for science have argued that modern science has demonstrated that belief in God is no longer credible. A spate of bestselling books, led by Richard Dawkins's *The God Delusion*, have popularized this idea. Dawkins and other New Atheists argue that science shows the existence of God to be a delusion, "a failed hypothesis" as one book suggests. Why? Because, according to them, there is no evidence for intelligent design. Instead, in their

* Originally published in the *CSB Apologetics Study Bible* under the same title.

view, Charles Darwin explained away all evidences of design. Indeed, the modern version of Darwin's theory, Neo-Darwinism, asserts that the wholly undirected processes of natural selection and random mutations is fully capable of producing the intricate structures in living systems. As Dawkins asserts, natural selection can mimic the powers of a designing intelligence without itself being guided or directed by an intelligent agent of any kind. Thus, living organisms may look designed, but in his view, that appearance is illusory. Since, he says, the design argument was always prior to Darwin the strongest argument for God's existence, the idea of a Creator is now extremely improbable—and placing faith in him is tantamount to choosing a delusion.

But is the premise of Dawkins's argument accurate? Has Darwinism refuted the design hypothesis and, with it, any scientific evidence for the existence of God?

In fact Darwinism has not disproved the case for intelligent design, and the foundational premise of Dawkins's argument is fatally flawed. Today there is compelling evidence of intelligent design within the inner recesses of the simplest living cells. Darwin didn't know about this evidence and neither Darwin's theory, nor modern Neo-Darwinism, even addresses it.

Darwin attempted to explain the origin of new living forms as starting from simpler preexisting forms of life. But he did not explain, or even attempt to explain, the origin of life's building basic block—the simplest living cells.

Biologists committed to the Darwinian perspective with its denial of design were not initially troubled by this gap in materialistic explanation. During the late nineteenth century they thought the cell was an extremely simple "glob of plasma." Such an entity, they thought, could have formed readily from a few simple undirected chemical reactions without any designing hand's involvement.

But as biologists gradually learned more about the complexity of the cell, evolutionary theorists devised increasingly more sophisticated theories of chemical evolution—theories that attempt to explain the origin of the first life arising gradually from simpler preexisting chemicals. Nevertheless, all such theories began to encounter severe problems after the 1950s as scientists began to learn more about the complexity of cells and the information-rich molecules contained within them.

In 1953, when James Watson and Francis Crick elucidated the structure of the DNA molecule, they announced a startling discovery. The structure of DNA allows it to store information in the form of a four-character digital code. Strings of precisely sequenced chemicals called nucleotide bases store and transmit the assembly instructions—the information—for building the crucial protein molecules and machines each cell needs to survive.

Crick later developed this idea with his famous sequence hypothesis, according to which the chemical constituents in DNA function like letters in a written language or symbols in a computer code. Just as English letters may convey a particular message depending on their arrangement, so too do certain sequences of chemical bases along the spine of a DNA molecule convey precise instructions for building proteins. The arrangement of the chemical characters determines the function of the sequence as a whole. Thus, the DNA molecule has the same property of sequence specificity that characterizes codes and language. As Dawkins himself has acknowledged, "The machine code of the genes is uncannily computer-like." Or, as Bill Gates has noted, "DNA is like a computer program, but far, far more advanced than any software we've ever created."

After the early 1960s, further discoveries made clear that the digital information in DNA and RNA is only part of a complex information processing system innate within the cell. It's an advanced form of nanotechnology that both mirrors and exceeds our own in its complexity, design logic, and information storage density.

So where did the digital information in the cell originate? And how did the cell's complex information processing system arise? Clearly, the informational features of the cell at least appear designed. To date, no theory of undirected chemical evolution has explained the origin of the digital information needed to build the first living cell. There is, it turns out, simply too much information housed within the cell to be explained away by chance alone. Moreover, the information in DNA has also been shown to defy explanation by reference to the laws of chemistry. Saying otherwise would be like claiming that a clever newspaper headline could arise as the result of the chemical attraction between ink and paper. Clearly something else is at work.

Importantly, scientists arguing for intelligent design do not do so merely because natural processes—chance, laws, or the combination of the two—have failed to explain the origin of the information-rich systems in cells. Rather, they argue for design because experience teaches that systems possessing such features invariably arise from intelligent causes. The information on a computer screen can be traced back to a user or programmer. The information in a book ultimately came from a writer. As the pioneering information theorist Henry Quastler observed, "Information habitually arises from conscious activity."

To summarize, DNA functions like a software program. We know from experience that software comes from programmers. We know generally that information— whether inscribed in hieroglyphics or encoded in a radio signal—always arises from an intelligent source. The discovery of information in the DNA molecule, therefore, provides strong grounds for inferring that a designing intelligence played a role in the origin of DNA as well as life itself.

Thus, contrary to the New Atheists who claim there is no evidence of actual design in life—which, in their view renders belief in God untenable—the DNA molecule reveals powerful evidence of a designing mind's work. Neither Darwinism, nor Richard Dawkins and the New Atheists, have disproved the design hypothesis or the existence of God.

CAN EVOLUTION EXPLAIN ETHICS?*

Mark Linville

Charles Darwin thought that the universal human tendency to think in terms of moral rightness and wrongness, and our wide agreement on the immorality of acts like rape or genocide, could be explained by the evolution of the human species. Given the circumstances of survival and reproduction, he theorized, some behaviors are more adaptive than others; thus, any instinct that prompts adaptive behaviors is favored by natural selection. The flight instinct removes prey from

---

* Originally published in the *CSB Apologetics Study Bible* under the same title.

the clutches of predators, increasing the chances that the pursued creature will live to reproduce. Social animals such as bees, wolves, and people come equipped with sets of social instincts that prompt cooperation with the hive, pack, or tribe. The success of the more cooperative group, whether it is competing with other tribes, hunting, or gathering, tends to promote the survival and reproduction of its individual members. To the extent that such cooperative and adaptive behavior is genetically fostered, he believed, it tends to be passed on to offspring: natural selection at work on the human psyche.

True, bees seem programmed automatically to act from purely social instincts, but any social animal also endowed with intellectual powers—like those at work in people—would be capable of *reflection* upon those instincts, too. The female wolf instinctually cares for her cubs without moral reflection because of the evolutionary advantage of such instinctual behavior. The human mother, however, is driven by a similar instinctual impulse that is bolstered by the sense that it would be wrong of her to abandon or neglect her babies: she has a conscience. For Darwin, what is called "conscience" is merely the product of social instincts plus a capacity for rational reflection. In his estimation, then, human morality is the product of natural selection shaping and honing human psychology—which is also influenced by individuals interacting with the circumstances of human culture over the eons.

All of this may explain why people have come to believe that there are such things as right and wrong acts, but it utterly fails to explain how there could actually be an objective difference between right and wrong. Indeed, the explanation undermines those beliefs, because given the supposed circumstances of evolution, humans would have believed them whether true or false. Darwin's theory requires that our moral sense—and its dictates—evolved simply because the behavior it encourages is adaptive.

Whether the resulting moral beliefs are also true is beside the point. This has led some proponents of Darwin's account to observe that ethics is "an illusion fobbed off on us by our genes to get us to cooperate."

What is missing from Darwin's theory is any reason for thinking that, in addition to being adaptive, human moral faculties aim at producing moral beliefs that are true as they would be were they designed for the purpose of establishing moral truth within the fiber of society. Without that background assumption, which is the sort afforded us in the Genesis creation account, we should all be moral nihilists. In short, when combined with an atheistic outlook, Darwin's theory does not explain ethics; it explains it away.

DOES SCIENCE SUPPORT THE BIBLE?*

Walter L. Bradley

Introduction

T wo major areas of scientific inquiry can in principle either support or undermine the Bible, namely, what science tells us about the nature of our universe and planet and what it can tell us about the history of our universe and planet. Biblical theism describes a God who is immediately responsible for all physical reality, with the laws of nature seen as descriptions of God's customary way of caring for his creatures (as in Col 1:17). Biblical theism also affirms that God sometimes works

* Originally published in the *CSB Apologetics Study Bible* under the same title.

in extraordinary (or supernatural) ways to shape and care for his creation (Gn 1:1). The challenge is, can the biblical and scientific pictures of our universe and planet be harmonized?

Our Remarkable Home

One of the most surprising scientific developments of the twentieth and early twenty-first centuries has been the discovery of the many remarkable features of our universe and planet that are essential to make it such an ideal habitat for life. First, we need a sufficient diversity of elements, combined with a relative abundance of certain critical elements, to make possible the production of complex "molecular machines" capable of processing energy, storing information, and replicating molecules such as RNA, DNA, and protein. Second, at least one element in this complexity of life must be capable of serving as a ready connector, reacting with essentially all elements to form bonds that are stable but not too stable to be broken during "reuse"; carbon is such an element. Third, we must have an individual element or compound that is liquid at certain temperatures on planet earth and very abundant and that can serve as a universal solvent. This liquid must be capable of dissolving most elements and/or compounds essential to the chemistry of life; that describes water. Fourth, we need long-term sources of energy that fit with the chemical energy in the carbon bonds so that this energy can fuel the chemical reactions we find in the carbon-based, chain molecules that are essential to life.

At least fifty such requirements have been identified, all necessary for life to exist in our universe.

God's Remarkable Design

God has satisfied the many requirements for life in three remarkable ways: the elegant mathematical form that is encoded in nature and that we call "the laws of nature"; the fine-tuning of the nineteen universal constants (e.g., the speed of light, the gravity force constant, the mass of the electron, and the unit charge); and the unbelievably demanding initial conditions that God had to set. For example, the ratio of the strong force constant to the electromagnetic force constant must fall within a window of five percent of the actual ratio if we are to have elemental diversity and a star like our sun that gives a long-term, stable source of energy. To match the energy of the light from the sun to the chemical bonding energy in organic compounds, six of the universal constants have to be carefully tailored to each other. The speed of light (c), the mass of the electron (m_e), the mass of the proton (m_p), Planck's constant (h), the gravity force constant, and the unit charge must have carefully matched magnitudes that satisfy the following algebraic equation:

$$m_p{}^2 \cdot G/[h\ c] > \sim [e^2/\{hc\}]^{12}[me/mp]^4$$

Remarkably, these six constants do have exactly the right relative values for the energy from the sun to be matched precisely to that needed to facilitate critical chemical reactions in organic molecules.

Many scientists have remarked with admiration about this amazing characteristic of our universe. For example, the famous English astronomer Sir Fred Hoyle commented, "A common sense interpretation of the facts suggests that a super intellect has 'monkeyed' with the physics as well as the chemistry and biology, and there are no blind forces worth speaking about in nature."

Possibly the most impressive scientific achievement of

twentieth century was the discovery of DNA, upon which is encoded the information of life. That such a remarkable information storage system exists, and that the DNA molecules have somehow come to be encoded with the precise information needed for life, is the climax to an amazing testimony from science of God's providential care for us in his creation. For example, for the accidental origin of the cytochrome-C molecule to have the required sequencing of the various amino acids has a probability of only 1 in 10^{60}.

These findings from recent science give an even more profound significance to Paul's testimony in Rm 1:20 that God's divinity can be seen even in the invisible elements of his universe.

Can We Harmonize Genesis 1 and Science?

While the scientific discoveries of the twentieth and twenty-first centuries have strengthened belief in a Designer/Creator, highly publicized conflicts between science and the Bible such as the Scopes "Monkey Trial" have eroded confidence in the biblical inferences about natural history found in Genesis 1–2. This conflict is the result of unsubstantiated scientific claims and unnecessarily limited interpretations of Genesis 1–2 (whether they be of the liberal or conservative variety).

The unsupported claim from science is that the origin of life and its progression from simple to complex forms are achieved by molecular selection and mutation/natural selection respectively. While this synthesis of mutation/natural selection adequately explains how organisms become more adapted to their environment and how incremental improvement in existing characteristics might occur, it seems incapable of explaining the origin of multicomponent systems, such as the human eye. New multicomponent systems would have no advantage from natural selection until the individual parts had already evolved to an advanced stage of development. Yet without natural selection to guide this development, it is almost impossible to imagine how complex, multicomponent systems can originate. Biochemist Michael Behe has dubbed this process "Darwin's black box"—a whimsical term for a device that does something but whose inner workings cannot be seen and sometimes are not comprehensible.

HOW SHOULD A CHRISTIAN RELATE TO A SCIENTIFIC NATURALIST?*

J. P. Moreland

"I'm too scientific for religious superstition. Science is the only way of gaining knowledge of reality, and it tells us the physical world is all there is." This claim, espoused by scientific naturalists, is called *scientism*, the view that science is the paradigm of truth and rationality.

There are two forms of scientism: strong and weak. *Strong scientism* implies that something is true if and only if it is a scientific claim that has been successfully tested

---

* Originally published in the *CSB Apologetics Study Bible* under the same title.

and used according to appropriate scientific methodology. Within this view there are no truths apart from scientific truths, and even if there were, there would be no reason to believe them.

Weak scientism allows for truths to exist apart from science and grants them some minimal rational status without scientific support. Still, weak scientism implies that science is the most authoritative sector of human learning.

If either form is true, drastic implications result for theology. If strong scientism is true, then theology is not a cognitive enterprise at all and there is no such thing as theological knowledge. If weak scientism is true, then the conversation between theology and science will be a monologue, with theology listening to science and waiting for its support.

What, then, should we say about scientism, and what should Christians say to those who hold this belief?

Note first that strong scientism is self-refuting. Strong scientism is not itself a proposition *of* science but a proposition of philosophy *about* science to the effect that only scientific propositions are true and/or rational.

And strong scientism is itself offered as a true, rationally justified position. Propositions that are self-refuting do not just happen to be false; they are necessarily false—it is not possible for them to be true. No future progress will have the slightest effect on making strong scientism more acceptable.

Two more problems count equally against strong and weak scientism. First, scientism does not adequately allow for the task of stating and defending the necessary presuppositions for science itself to be practiced. Thus scientism shows itself to be a foe and not a friend of science. Science cannot be practiced in thin air. Scientism has many assumptions, each has been challenged, and the task of stating and defending these assumptions is a philosophical one. The conclusions of science cannot be more certain than the presuppositions it rests upon and uses to reach those conclusions.

Strong scientism rules out these presuppositions altogether because neither the presuppositions themselves nor their defense are scientific matters. Weak scientism misconstrues its strength because it believes that scientific propositions have greater intellectual authority than those of other fields, such as philosophy. This would mean that the conclusions of science are more certain than the philosophical presuppositions used to justify and reach those conclusions, and that is absurd.

Here are some of the philosophical presuppositions of science:

- the existence of a theory of an independent, external world
- the orderly nature of the external world
- the knowability of the external world
- the existence of truth
- the existence of the laws of logic
- the reliability of our cognitive and sensory faculties to serve as truth gatherers and as a source of justified beliefs in our intellectual environment
- the adequacy of language to describe the world
- and the existence of values used in science (e.g., "Test theories fairly and report test results honestly").

Second, there are true, rational beliefs in fields outside science. Strong scientism does not allow for this fact, and it is therefore to be rejected as an account of our intellectual enterprise.

Moreover, some claims outside science (for instance, "Torturing babies is wrong" or "I am now thinking about science") are better justified than some believed within science (for example, "Evolution takes place through a series of very small steps"). It is not hard to believe that many of our currently held scientific beliefs will and should be revised or abandoned in a hundred years, but it would be hard to see how the same could be said of the nonscientific propositions just cited. Weak scientism does not account for this fact.

In sum, scientism in both forms is inadequate, and it is important for Christians to integrate science and theology with genuine respect for both.

HAS NEUROSCIENCE UNDERMINED WARRANT FOR BELIEVING IN THE SOUL?*

J. P. Moreland

Today, many believe the findings of neuroscience have undermined the rationality for believing in the soul. But no matter how often that idea is verbalized, nothing could be further from the truth. Why? Because if the soul is an immaterial substance containing consciousness (sensations, emotions, thoughts, beliefs, desires, acts of free will) and also animates the body and gives it life, then the methods and findings of neuroscience are almost

---

* Originally published in the *CSB Apologetics Study Bible* under the same title.

entirely irrelevant to questions about the nature and existence of consciousness and the soul.

Different fields of study—art, psychology, logic, physics, ethics, history, philosophy, neuroscience—employ varied methods to study different objects, yet they provide knowledge of their appropriate subject matter. For example, the methods of logic and math vary from those employed in chemistry, and logic and math are used to study different objects than those investigated in a laboratory. Branches of human knowledge, then, have their limits; they are set by other branches of knowledge. Specifically, the limits of science in general, and neuroscience in particular, make them inadequate to elucidate the nature and existence of consciousness and the soul. These matters are objects of theological and philosophical knowledge, not of neuroscience.

To illustrate, consider the notion of empirically equivalent theories. When two theories are consistent with the same empirical data, they are empirically equivalent. Take, for example, Neo-Darwinism versus Punctuated Equilibrium Theory (the view that physical objects retain their size over time versus the notion that the size of objects doubles hourly as does the size of our measuring instruments). In such a case, empirical, scientific considerations cannot be used to adjudicate between the rivals. Instead, more philosophical considerations like simplicity and explanatory power must be considered.

Now, consider three theories about consciousness and the self. First, strict physicalism holds that conscious states like pains or thoughts are really nothing but physical states in the brain; moreover, it states that no self exists beyond the brain or body. The human person is entirely physical. Second, property dualism holds that no self exists beyond the brain or body, but conscious states are genuinely and irreducibly mental, not physical states: both are contained in the brain. Third, substance dualism holds that physical states, like certain neurons firing, are in the brain while mental states, like a feeling of pain caused by firing neurons, are in the soul.

These three theories are, strictly speaking, empirically equivalent. For example, consider mirror neurons, which must fire in the right way in order for someone to experience empathy for another. The three empirically equivalent theories account for this: mirror-neuron firing is identical to a feeling of empathy (strict physicalism); mirror neurons are physical states that cause the mental state of feeling empathy, and both states are in the brain (property dualism); mirror neurons are physical states in the brain that cause the mental state of feeling empathy in the soul (substance dualism). Property and substance dualists accept correlations, causal connections, and dependency relations between physical and mental states; for example, brain damage can keep one from recalling memories. Nonetheless, this does not prove they are identical nor does it prove that physical states and mental states occur in the same owner.

After all, if a person is locked into the driver's seat of a car, he is dependent on the car to move. If the steering wheel is broken, allowing only right turns, this does not prove that the driver is the car, but that while he is *in* the car, he depends on its functioning parts. Similarly, while in his body, the individual needs certain organs—eyes, ears, and brain—to function properly lest his mental functioning be impeded. Neuroscience can only show correlations, causal relations, or functional dependencies between mental states and physical states, between the self/soul and the brain/body. In the 1200s, Thomas

Aquinas said that a damaged brain would limit one's thinking; neuroscience has only made this observation more precise.

The irrelevance of neuroscience and the centrality of theology and philosophy for clarifying issues of consciousness and the self can be easily seen in the following, typical questions in philosophy of mind that neuroscience cannot answer.

First, they cannot answer ontological questions like these: To what is a mental or physical property identical? To what is a mental or physical event identical? To what is the owner of mental properties/events identical? What is a human person? How are mental properties related to mental events? Are there essences and, if so, what is the essence of a mental event or of a human person? Is a man essentially a human, a person, or both?

Second, they cannot answer epistemological questions like these: How do we obtain knowledge or justified beliefs about other minds and about our own minds? Is there a proper epistemic order to first-person knowledge of one's own mind and third-person knowledge of other minds? How reliable is first-person introspection, and what is its nature? If reliable, should first-person introspection be limited to providing knowledge about mental states, or should it be extended to include knowledge of one's ego?

Third, they cannot answer semantic questions like these: What is a meaning? What is a linguistic entity, and how is it related to a meaning? Is thought reducible to or a necessary condition for language use? How do the terms in our common-sense psychological vocabulary get their meaning?

And fourth, they cannot answer methodological questions. How should one proceed in analyzing and resolving the first-order issues that constitute the philosophy of mind? What is the proper order between philosophy and science? Should we adopt some form of philosophical naturalism, set aside so-called first philosophy, and engage topics in the philosophy of mind within a framework of our empirically best-attested theories relevant to those topics? What is the role of thought experiments in the philosophy of mind, and how does the first-person point of view factor into generating the materials for formulating those thought experiments?

Neuroscience is a wonderful field of study, but like other fields, it has limitations.

DOES THE BIBLE PROVIDE GUIDANCE REGARDING GENETIC ENGINEERING?*

Scott B. Rae

S ince human beings weren't able to manipulate the genetic code when the Bible was written, it doesn't directly address genetic engineering. It does, however, give general principles regarding medical technology that apply to genetic technologies.

Humans are created in God's image and likeness, and so he charges them to exercise dominion over his creation (Gn 1:27–28). Their mandate? To subdue and

---

* Originally published in the *CSB Apologetics Study Bible* under the same title.

kindly master the earth, unlocking its resources to benefit themselves and their successors—in a sense continuing the spirit of creation by being subordinate "creators" with God in unlocking the secrets of the creation to benefit humankind.

The command to subdue the earth takes on added complexity after the entrance of sin into the world in Genesis 3. Exercising dominion over creation after the fall now involves dealing with sin's effects in the world. Dominion includes working toward improving the creation or reversing the effects of the entrance of sin. The most important of sin's effects is the reality of death (Gn 3:2–3), which is universal in its scope (Rm 5:12). That is, after the fall, death, decay, and deterioration face every person. Thus dominion over creation largely involves dealing with death and disease (disease being the cause of death in most cases), which can alleviate the harshness of life after the fall, even genetic disease. In order to exercise dominion God (through general revelation) provided human beings with resources necessary for accomplishing that task. That ingenuity and wisdom come from God as his "common grace" gifts to humans (Is 28:23–29).

The knowledge and skill necessary to develop the kinds of technologies that enable humankind to subdue the creation are part of God's general revelation. Humans didn't acquire the ingenuity and skill to develop sophisticated technology on their own apart from God. It's not an accident that these technologies came to be so useful in our exercise of dominion over creation. They are gifts from God. Thus technologies that generally improve the lot of humanity and specifically help reverse the effects of sin's entrance into the world are part of God's common grace. The skill and expertise needed to bring about these creation-subduing technologies come ultimately from God, being his good gifts to humans in harnessing creation.

This is particularly the case when it comes to medical technology. Since death is one of the primary consequences of the entrance of sin into the world, and disease is the primary cause of death and physical deterioration, medical technologies bringing cures to diseases and other afflictions are among God's most gracious gifts to the human race.

Medical technology can be part of God's common

grace to assist humans in fulfilling their role in exercising loving dominion. The more controversial technology of genetic engineering should be used only for therapeutic reasons (repairing damage), in keeping with the creation mandate. It should not be used for eugenic reasons (creating a kind of super race, as Hitler and the Nazis hoped to do, considering other races inferior to the so-called Aryans). C. S. Lewis warned that if "the dreams of some scientific planners are realized" by using their power to make their descendants into what they please, then their "conquest of Nature . . . means the rule of a few hundreds of men over billions upon billions of men."

CAN GOD'S ACTIONS BE DETECTED SCIENTIFICALLY?*

C. John Collins

"I 'll believe in God if you can prove scientifically that he does things!" How can we respond to such a challenge?

The first thing we must do is disentangle the questions involved here. First, what do we mean by "God's actions"? Second, what do we mean by "science"? And third, can science detect events as *God's* actions? Let's take them one at a time.

To begin with, we recognize that, after the creation,

---

* Originally published in the *CSB Apologetics Study Bible* under the same title.

God works in two ways. First, he maintains the things
he created, along with their powers to cause things.
Apples keep on tasting good and nourishing us because
God keeps maintaining their properties. A soccer goalie
deflects the ball because God maintains the properties of
the ball, the air, and the goalie's body. Second, God is not
limited by the powers of created things. Sometimes he
goes beyond their powers if it suits his purpose. We can
call the first kind of action the *natural* (since it works
with created natures) and the second the *supernatural*
(since it goes beyond natural powers). Let's be clear
about this: *Both* kinds are God's actions and both serve
his purpose.

The sciences study aspects of the world around us in
hopes of understanding how they work. Some scientists
study the regularities of the world (such as "the angle of
incidence equals the angle of reflection"), while others
study specific events, trying to reason backward from
effect to cause (like Sherlock Holmes, the "scientific
detective").

Can God's actions be detected scientifically? It depends
on which ones. Because God made his world "very good"

(Gn 1:31), it needs no tinkering to keep in operation, so we don't expect that the sciences will "detect" God's natural actions. The reason that an atom's electrons don't crash into the nucleus is not that God holds them apart by a miracle but that he made their properties so that they don't crash.

On the other hand, the sciences may sometimes help us detect a supernatural event because in knowing the properties of natural things, we can tell when these have been transcended. For example, the more we know about how babies come about, the more clearly supernatural becomes the conception of Jesus: There is no natural explanation for it. As C. S. Lewis put it, "No doubt a modern gynecologist knows several things about birth and begetting which St. Joseph did not know. But these things do not concern the main point—that a virgin birth is contrary to the course of nature. And St. Joseph obviously knew *that*." Advances in medical science have only sharpened the point. We could say the same about Jesus's resurrection: Dead bodies stay dead unless someone with extraordinary power interferes.

This kind of detection works best when it's based on knowledge, not ignorance. It's not just that we don't know how it could happen; rather, we have every reason to believe that it *can't* happen unless something else is added. The sciences can help us to know better the natures of the things involved and thus to know when "something else" is needed to explain what we see.

WHAT IS A BIBLICAL BASIS FOR SCIENCE?*

John A. Bloom

A popular myth in our culture says that science and theology have always been at war with each other. It may come as a surprise to learn that most historians of science believe this idea to be untrue. In fact, the Bible provided some of the key intellectual foundations for the development of the sciences in the West.

God as Master of the Universe

The first foundation is the expectation of regularity in

* Originally published in the *CSB Worldview Study Bible* under the title "A Biblical Basis for Science."

nature, which stems from the Bible's monotheistic view of God. Polytheistic and pantheistic religions see the universe as run by committee, with unpredictable events arising from conflicts among the many supernatural personalities involved. As a result, nature is seen as capricious, without any expectation of regularity.

By contrast, the Bible presents God as the sole Master and Commander of the universe (Ps 89:11–13; Is 48:12–13) which he spoke into existence (Pss 33:6–9; 148:5) and over which he rules (Is 40:26). Since one God is in control of nature and has said that he does not change (Nm 23:19; Mal 3:6), we can expect his universe to run in a regular way. This is more than an inference: God explicitly says that he established the heavens and earth to follow regular laws (Gn 8:22; Jr 33:20,25).

Science as a Worthy Pursuit

Another foundation is the Bible's teaching that the study of nature is a worthy pursuit in gaining wisdom and glorifying God. God's creation is good, and even though it is corrupted by sin, we are encouraged to learn from it

(Ps 19:1; Pr 6:6). Psalm 104 and Job 38–39 praise God's wisdom, sovereignty, and control over creation.

Scientists such as Isaac Newton and Johannes Kepler often stated that they sought to glorify God by studying his creation. In his letter to the Grand Duchess Christina, Galileo remarked, "The glory and greatness of Almighty God are marvelously discerned in all His works and divinely read in the open book of Heaven." By contrast, many world religions view nature in a dualistic manner, regarding the spiritual world as good and the material world as evil. So studying the physical world focuses one's attention in the wrong direction.

The Complexity of God's World

A third biblical foundation for science is that God's creation is not simple to understand. God informs us that "[His] thoughts are not [our] thoughts, and [our] ways are not [his] ways" (Is 55:8; see also Pr 25:2). Yet "The LORD founded the earth by wisdom and established the heavens by understanding" (Pr 3:19). This suggests that through difficult work we may be able to glimpse some of

God's wisdom. When doing science, as Kepler quipped, we are "thinking God's thoughts after Him."

God's Contingency

The last foundation to mention here is God's contingency: God created the world as he wanted it to be; he was not bound by outside constraints like human logic or philosophical principles. God "does whatever he pleases in heaven and on earth, in the seas and all the depths" (Ps 135:6; see also 115:3). Therefore, we cannot predict how God created; we must study God's handiwork itself to see what he has done. Thus, good science is based on direct observations and experiments while theories are held tentatively until proven beyond doubt.

Tensions Between Science and Theology

While the Bible is not a scientific textbook, we find that it provides the correct perspectives for viewing nature and the proper motivations for studying it. Science is arguably one of the tasks mankind is commissioned to do: Adam was to "name" the animals in the garden of Eden (Gn 2:19), and he was given stewardship over the earth (Gn 1:28), a task that required study and wisdom for it to be done well. Although the Bible has higher priorities than explaining how the heavens work, biblical descriptions of nature are profoundly true while simply stated. Examples are the creation event in Genesis 1:1 (see also Is 44:24; Heb 11:3), and the heavens and the earth's wearing out over time (Ps 102:25–26), an echo of the second law of thermodynamics.

If the study of nature was historically grounded in biblical insights, how did the modern tensions between science and theology arise? The drift started in the late 1600s when the philosophers of the Enlightenment freed themselves from the shackles of Aristotle and other ancient authorities by attempting to rely only on reason and experience to establish truth claims. Newton's discovery of the laws of motion and gravity led philosophers and theologians away from a theistic view (where God is actively involved in nature) to a deistic view (where God created the universe but now allows it to operate via laws he established). In the 1800s, T. H. Huxley and others desired to ground all knowledge on physical cause and effect, removing religious authority from society and replacing it with the authority of science. This narrowed the practice of science, limiting it to purely naturalistic explanations of the world.

Thus, the issues between the sciences and theology today hinge on the religious differences between naturalism and theism. In other words, should we view the universe as purely a machine which God cannot touch, or as a musical instrument which God plays for his glory? The difference is profound with respect to the explanations we can accept for natural phenomena. For example, if naturalism is assumed, something like Darwinism must be the "scientific" explanation for how life developed, because God's guidance or intervention in nature is ruled out *a priori*. Any naturalistic explanation must be preferred, no matter how implausible it is, because others would not be naturalistic. Unfortunately, by ignoring some possible answers, science today may be missing the truth. This is perhaps most evident in the fields of biology, psychology, and the social sciences where the abandonment of man's special place in creation in favor of explaining him as a machine or an animal has led to the devaluing of human life and personhood.

Strikingly, this philosophical shift in the foundation of science from theism to naturalism leaves people with little justification to pursue science. Better technology can earn one fame and fortune, a military advantage, or more comfortable living, but naturalistically minded scientists have no reason to expect mathematics to explain and predict how the universe behaves, no reason to expect the world to operate in a regular manner, and no explanation for what put the "material" in materialism in the first place. The *ad hoc* nature of the naturalistic presupposition has become more glaring with the recognition that our universe is not eternal but had a beginning and that the physical laws and constants themselves appear to be fine-tuned to allow for the possibility of complex, intelligent life. Naturalists sometimes suggest that our universe is just one among countless universes in a so-called multiverse, and that with so many universes the chances were good that at least one would turn out to be fine-tuned for life. But importantly, there is no evidence indicating that other universes exist.

Christians and Science

Is it possible for the sciences to return to a biblical basis? Certainly for Christians it is. We should look beyond the naturalistic, materialistic, and mechanistic blinders that limit the perspective of our culture, choosing to see that "the world is charged with the grandeur of God" (Gerard Manley Hopkins, "God's Grandeur"). Christians who marvel at the wisdom, power, and creativity demonstrated in God's handiwork, as the biblical writers and early scientists did, have a strong motive to pursue the sciences even if their colleagues espouse a narrower viewpoint.

The fine-tuning of our universe and the fact that it had a beginning strongly imply that Someone is behind it. So too does the dizzying complexity of life, which is becoming more evident as biochemistry unravels the secrets of life. If, through continued discoveries like these, the naturalistic straitjacket on valid scientific explanations comes to be seen for what it is—a theologically motivated restriction—perhaps science will soon shed naturalism, just as it shed its Aristotelian and Platonic straitjackets in the past. Perhaps then it will return to its theistic roots—the most fruitful perspective for viewing nature.

HOW TO NAVIGATE THE DISCUSSION ON EVOLUTION AND INTELLIGENT DESIGN?*

William A. Dembski

U ntil two centuries years ago, evolution played a negligible role in the Christian worldview. Christians overwhelmingly believed that God created the world and specially designed the different kinds of organisms that populate it. The diversity of life was therefore not seen as the result of a long evolutionary history, in which organisms gradually transformed into others that looked nothing like their beginnings. Any change in

* Originally published in the *CSB Worldview Study Bible* under the title "Evolution and Intelligent Design".

organisms from the original creation would have been minor. Insofar as there was any evolution, it would have been microevolution (changes within a species), not macroevolution (changes from one species to another).

Fast-forward to the present, and we find Christians having little choice but to square evolution with their worldview. For some, evolution is a proven fact incompatible with Christianity, causing them to reject the faith. For others, "theistic evolutionists," evolution is a proven fact but compatible with Christianity. For still others, evolution is incompatible with Christianity but so unsupported by evidence that it poses no direct challenge to Christian faith. Nevertheless, even those who think evolution is unconvincing must confront those who think it is well supported.

The Two Pillars of Evolution

To see why evolution is such a sticky issue for the Christian worldview, we need to be clear what the term *evolution* means. Evolution, as taught in biology textbooks, rests on two pillars. The first is a claim about natural history, according to which all living forms trace their lineage back to a common universal ancestor. This pillar of evolution is called common descent. By itself, common descent is compatible with theism in that God might, via an evolutionary process, bring all organisms into existence. Where common descent runs into trouble is with a biblical theism that takes Genesis seriously and sees God as creating the basic kinds of organisms from nothing.

The much more controversial pillar of evolution is the mechanism by which organisms are supposed to have arisen. To say that organisms have evolved raises an immediate question: how? In our experience, like begets like, so to say that organisms are able to change radically needs an explanation. Charles Darwin offered such an explanation, and it remains the explanation evolutionary theorists offer to this day. That explanation is natural selection, a process taking place over long periods of time. This is the second pillar of evolution.

Here is how natural selection works. When organisms reproduce, they don't form exact copies of themselves. If they did, there could be no evolution since offspring would be replicas of their parents. Organisms, when they reproduce, vary. Some variants are better adapted to their environments than others. Those that are well adapted will be selected for; those that are not will be selected against. That's a nice way of saying that some will get to live and reproduce, and others will be killed off within a given ecosystem. Evolutionists believe that over time natural selection is the invisible hand that shapes all life.

The point that Christians need to realize about natural selection is that at no place does this mechanism require the help of an intelligent agent. Quite the contrary. Evolutionist Francisco Ayala is on record as saying that Darwin's greatest achievement was to show how the apparent design of organisms could be achieved without actual design. Darwin himself, in commenting on his theory in a letter to Charles Lyle, stated, "I would give nothing for the theory of natural selection if it requires miraculous additions at any one stage of descent." Darwin's theory doesn't so much claim that God had nothing to do with life; instead, it suggests life doesn't need anything from God.

Theistic Evolution Versus Intelligent Design

Theistic evolution takes these two pillars of evolution and baptizes them in a sense, saying that this is how God formed life. In this view, God rather than directly guiding the evolutionary process, sets up the conditions under which evolution can take place. This has a certain appeal, especially if one is convinced that evolution as outlined by Darwin has indeed occurred. But why should one think that it has? Theistic evolution attempts to make a place for evolution within a Christian worldview. But the only reason for doing so is if evolution deserves such a place. In fact, the evidence for macroevolution is weak.

How can one see that the evidence for evolution is tenuous? The work of intelligent design theorists has been pivotal in critiquing evolution. Intelligent design (ID) casts the debate over evolution not as a science-versus-religion controversy but as a science-versus-science controversy. Theistic evolutionists, for instance, regard evolution as overwhelmingly supported scientifically and then try to reconcile their faith with that supposed fact. ID, by contrast, simply tries to assess the scientific evidence for evolution and design. If, as ID theorists argue, evolution fails, then there is no point trying to reconcile evolution and Christianity.

What, then, is ID and what makes it such an effective

tool against evolution? Intelligent design is, by definition, the study of patterns in nature that are best explained as the product of intelligence. Many special sciences fall under ID, including archaeology (Is that an arrowhead or a random chunk of rock?) and the search for extraterrestrial intelligence (Is that radio signal from outer space a message or mere noise?). Where ID becomes especially interesting is when the intelligence in view could not be the product of evolution. That happens with life because any intelligence responsible for life would be prior to life and thus not a product of evolution.

This point is crucial. Even though evolution is thought to produce intelligent beings like us, intelligence itself does nothing to guide the evolutionary process. Natural selection, for instance, acts automatically, weeding out those organisms ill suited for an environment while keeping those that are better suited. Yet if life gives clear evidence of design, then any process by which we got here must itself be intelligently guided.

It follows that evolution and intelligent design contradict each other. It is logically possible that God could substantively guide the evolutionary process and thereby introduce design, but such a theory of "intelligent evolution" is not what evolutionists, whether atheistic or theistic, mean by evolution. The beauty of evolution is that a purely naturalistic evolutionary mechanism (natural selection) is supposed to procure all the benefits of design without actual design.

Intelligent design, by contrast, shows that evolution is unable to make good on this promise. How can we see this? ID, in looking for patterns in nature best explained by intelligence, finds that biology does indeed exhibit such patterns, in everything from the fossil record (see Stephen Meyer's *Darwin's Dilemma*) to molecular biology (see Michael Behe's *Darwin's Black Box*). Take molecular biology. The DNA inside every one of your cells is known to stretch out to six feet in length, yet it is packed inside a volume much smaller than a pin head. DNA represents the most efficient and reliable method of data storage we know. Yet this method of data storage is presupposed by all of life.

Information storage and processing is not the only thing going on inside cells. There are transportation and distribution systems, signal transduction circuitries, waste removal services, and even nanoengineered motors.

Our best metaphor for understanding the cell is as an automated city in which everything, down to the smallest detail, is precisely tuned and coordinated. We need to be engineers to understand what's going on inside the cell, and when we do, we find a level of engineering that far exceeds anything human engineers have attained or show any signs of attaining. But ID doesn't just stop with marveling at the intricacies of the cell. It also investigates how such systems might have originated and what obstacles their origin faces in the absence of intelligence.

The Bible teaches that God by wisdom created the world (Pr 3:19) and that this wisdom is clearly evident throughout creation (Rm 1:20). Evolution, by contrast, teaches that if God had anything to do with life, then he was a master of stealth and gave no evidence of it. If it were well supported, evolution would therefore pose a significant challenge to the Christian worldview. But, especially in light of intelligent design, there is good reason to think evolution is ill supported and therefore not a threat to the Christian understanding of creation. In particular, attempts to reconcile Christianity and evolution are well-intentioned, but ultimately not needed.

THE
APOLOGETICS
STUDY BIBLE

REAL QUESTIONS. STRAIGHT ANSWERS. STRONGER FAITH.

APOLOGETICS

STUDY BIBLE FOR

STUDENTS

Edited by Dr. Sean McDowell

 ApologeticsBible.com

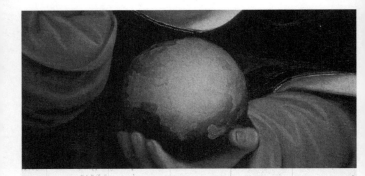

HOW
DO YOU
SEE THE
WORLD?

 CSBWorldviewStudyBible.com